A Story of
Saint John Vianney

A Story of Saint John Vianney

By
Brother Ernest, C.S.C.

Pictures by
Carolyn Lee Jagodits

Neumann Press
Charlotte, North Carolina

Nihil Obstat:
  C.F. Brooks, C.S.C.
    Censor Deputatus

Cum Permissu:
  Brother Donatus Schmitz, C.S.C
   Provincial

Imprimatur:
  ✝ Most Rev. Leo A. Pursley, D.D.
   Bishop of Fort Wayne–South Bend

A Story of St. John Vianney

ISBN 978-0-911845-30-3

Printed and bound in the United States of America.

Neumann Press
Charlotte, North Carolina
www.NeumannPress.com

2013

To Sister M. John Vianney

A STORY OF SAINT JOHN VIANNEY

Those of us who find it a little difficult to study should be very interested in a boy by the name of John Baptist Vianney. He was born in the town of Dardilly in France on May 8, 1786. His parents were farmers, and they had three other children before little John was born.

We know next to nothing about the other three Vianneys. They may have been real bright and got their lessons well. But we do know very much about little John, because he became a saint!

7

Matthew Vianney, little John's father, was very happy when the boy was born. He was thinking of the days when John would be old enough to care for the sheep. But Mother Vianney had other ideas. Right from the start, she felt John would become a priest. As soon as he was able to talk, she taught him to say the Our Father and Hail Mary.

One day, Mother Vianney took a little wooden statue of Our Lady down from the dresser and, holding it in front of her, told John the story of the Mother of Jesus. From that day, John cared nothing for his toys. If he could not carry the statue, he didn't bother about the toys.

And from that day, too, John held long talks with Our Lady. He told her his sorrows and joys, and his hopes for the future. And when he met any of his little friends, he tried his best to interest them in the story of Our Lady.

When other little children went along with John to the country, he would ask them to pray with him. Many times he had to teach these children the Our Father and Hail Mary. Their parents had not bothered to teach them!

In France, in those days, the Catholic churches and schools were all closed. Priests lived in fear of their lives.

In the town of Ecully, the birthplace of Matthew Vianney, some priests lived in hiding. Now and then the Vianneys would visit their relatives there and be able to hear Mass said in a home or a barn. It was during one of these visits that John made his first Confession. A year later, again in secret, he was able to make his First Communion. The Mass was said in a private home, early in the morning. All came at the risk of their lives. The government hated the Church and wanted to destroy it entirely.

But by the time John was seventeen, a new government was in power. Churches were opened, but there were now very few priests. John felt that he should become a priest. His mother agreed with him, but his father said he needed John's help on the farm for a few more years. So, John continued to work and pray for two more years.

At nineteen, John took his place with other, much younger, boys in a class taught by Father Balley. The younger boys learned fast; but John, in spite of his mighty efforts, his long prayers, his penances, could not keep up with them!

Discouraged, John spoke to Father Balley about giving up his studies for the priesthood. Father knew John was dull, but he told him to study!

John then made a sixty-mile trip on foot to the shrine of St. Francis Regis to beg of him the help he needed in his classes.

Then John was called into the army! He went to camp and at once became very sick. When he got well, he hurried to the church to pray for help in this new form of life. While he prayed, he forgot time. When he left the church he learned his army had gone hours before! He set out on foot to catch up. When darkness fell, he still saw nothing of his regiment. So, when a man in a little village asked him to stay for the night in his house, John accepted the invitation. And for fourteen months, John stayed in that home and went by the name of Jerome Vincent. Later he sent word to his folks who thought him dead because they had not heard from him for so long. They were wild with joy.

In those days it was possible to hire another person to take the place of one called into the army. So John's younger brother agreed to go. When John heard that, he came home at once and got a grand welcome from his family.

A few days later he returned to Father Balley who taught him privately. But the review of what he had learned was not finished before John got word to come home!

John found his mother very sick. A few days later she died. The parting was a great sorrow to the son she loved so well.

In November of 1812, Father Balley told John he was ready to begin the study of philosophy.

"I am sending you to the seminary in Lyons."

"O Father, I'm afraid I . . ."

"Trust in God, my son."

Well, John went to the seminary, but he failed to pass the entrance examination! Father Balley begged the superior to allow him to continue to teach John, and to give the boy an examination later on. The request was granted.

Months later, John came again to the seminary. The superior questioned him alone, and John answered very well.

"I shall accept you. God will do the rest. Pray hard and trust in Him!"

Four years later, in July of 1815, Bishop Simon agreed to ordain John, but only as a Mass priest, for John did not know enough moral theology to hear Confessions.

Months afterward, after long hours of daily study under Father Balley, Father John was given permission to hear Confessions, and his first penitent was the pastor, Father Balley!

Two years after this, Father Balley died and Father John Vianney was named pastor of the little town of Ars.

Father Vianney put his few possessions in a little cart and, with his old housekeeper, set out for Ars. He was to remain there for forty-two years! It was he who made the tiny town famous throughout the world.

The church was badly in need of repairs. It had been neglected through the years. Father soon saw that the rectory was too richly furnished to suit him. When he found the fancy things belonged to someone who lived in town, he sent them all back!

Father John soon found out that only a few came to Mass. The others were not interested in religion. Well, he would see to that. He would go into their homes for them!

Father dropped in on families right at meal time. He was not interested in getting something to eat, but he knew it was the only time he could find the families together.

And it wasn't long before the attendance at Mass increased. The men began to come. Father Vianney stressed the love of God in all of his sermons, and the need for Confession.

Next, the Cure of Ars, as Father Vianney was called, turned his attention to the children. He insisted they attend catechism classes, and he patiently taught them prayers and simple religious truths. He never tired of speaking of the love of God, and so sincere was he that the children loved to come to hear him. Soon the boys and girls, too, came to Mass and the sacraments.

But there were some people who did not like Father Vianney and what he was doing in Ars. Four of these were tavern owners. They soon found their business was falling off. People did not come to spend their money on drink. So these men went to Father John to protest.

"What is going to happen to our business?"

"That is something for you and the Devil to decide," Father told them.

Well, the Devil didn't help them, so the four taverns had to close. Three of the owners got other jobs, and the fourth, an old man, was taken care of by Father John. He got a little home for him with a plot of land, and the man made a good living by raising vegetables.

The next problem Father John had to handle was that of orphan girls. He bought a small house near the church and made it into an orphanage.

Three good women agreed to care for the girls. They taught them to sew, cook, read and write. Father Vianney came each day and very patiently taught them the catechism.

But the number of girls soon mounted to fifty. Father went from house to house to beg for money and food. People helped, but the problem became too great for Father Vianney to handle.

God worked many great miracles for poor Father Vianney so he would not have to close his orphanage. Father always prayed to St. Philomena and St. Francis Regis when he was in dire need of food, and help always came. Empty wheat bins filled up to the brim. Strangers brought large sums of money to him. The orphans never suffered any want!

By now the fame of the Cure of Ars had spread for many miles around. People came long distances to go to Confession to him. Many days he did not even have time to eat. He often began to hear Confessions at midnight and did so until time for Mass, and from then on until late into the night.

The people began to come to Father Vianney for him to cure them of sickness. And God often cured them through His faithful priest.

The Devil hated all the good Father Vianney was doing. He tried every way he could to frighten the poor priest. He kept him awake during the short time allowed for sleep by all sorts of loud noises in Father's house.

One night, the Devil dragged Father Vianney from his bed and threw him violently against the wall as if to kill him.

Next, the Devil tried to make Father Vianney believe that he gave so much of his time to the salvation of others that he was neglecting his own soul. Father worried very much about this and even begged his bishop to remove him from Ars and allow him to spend the remainder of his life in a monastery. But the bishop could not afford to lose the services of this holy priest. Twice Father John tried to run away during the night, but each time he did so, he found himself back again in the morning. Then he decided to remain at Ars no matter what might happen. God wanted him there.

Then Father Vianney became very sick with pneumonia. The doctor said he would surely die of it. But Father began to pray to Saint Philomena and Our Lady, and it was not long before the good priest got well.

The bishop then sent Father Vianney off for a rest with his brother in Dardilly. There he had but a few days of peace. News got around that the Cure of Ars was in Dardilly and a great crowd soon gathered to see and to talk to him.

When Father Vianney saw that his relatives were being upset by the crowds, he demanded that he be taken back to Ars.

For the next ten years, Father Vianney continued his regular work in Ars. That meant that he spent at least eighteen hours a day in the confessional. There was, too, the work at his orphanage, the visiting of the sick and dying.

Just how the good old priest was able to keep going on a crust of bread and some water, no one ever knew.

On July 29, 1859, the first signs of grave illness showed on Father Vianney. He fainted several times while getting ready to go to church.

His housekeeper heard a heavy noise in Father's room but got no response when she rapped on his door. She opened it and found poor Father Vianney, dressed in his worn cassock, lying unconscious on the floor. She hurried outside where many were in line waiting their turn to get inside the church and to the confessional. Two men went with her to Father's room. He was conscious at the time. He smiled a little and bade them welcome.

That evening Father sent for his confessor and made a general Confession. He was very peaceful. He showed no worry now about the salvation of his soul. He only looked forward to meeting the God he so dearly loved.

Four days later, the bishop and some of his priests arrived to be with Father Vianney during his last hours.

Great crowds of people gathered in the church and on the yard around the presbytery, and all prayed for the recovery of their great friend. They felt they could not part with him. No one could take his place.

But it was time for the holy priest to go to God to receive his great reward.

As Father Monnin prayed: "Let the holy angels of God come to meet him, and conduct him to the city of heavenly Jerusalem," Father John Vianney smiled calmly and died in peace. There was no sign of a struggle. A tired old man slept in the arms of God!

On November 1, 1934, the long Cause for the canonization of Father Vianney came to an end in St. Peter's in Rome when the great Pope Pius XI declared him a saint.

And in Ars today, in a great church built in his honor, thousands come to pay honor to the poor boy who had a hard time learning, but who became a great saint!

The End